THE FABULOUS LOST & FOUND

AND THE LITTLE MOUSE WHO SPOKE PORTUGUESE

WRITTEN BY MARK PALLIS
ILLUSTRATED BY PETER BAYNTON

NEU WESTEND
— PRESS —

For Oscar and Francisco - MP

For Hannah and Skye - PB

First Printing, 2020
ISBN: 978-1-913595-23-4
NeuWestendPress.com

THE FABULOUS LOST & FOUND

AND THE LITTLE MOUSE WHO SPOKE PORTUGUESE

WRITTEN BY MARK PALLIS
ILLUSTRATED BY PETER BAYNTON

NEU WESTEND
— PRESS —

In the middle of the big city is a tiny
yellow building. If anyone loses anything, this is
where it ends up.

It is called the Lost and Found.

Mr and Mrs Frog keep everything safe, hoping that someday every lost watch and bag and phone and toy and shoe and cheesegrater will find its owner again.

But the shop is very small. And there are so many lost things. It is all quite a squeeze, but still, it's fabulous.

One sunny day, a little mouse walked in.

"Welcome," said Mrs Frog. "What have you lost?"

"Perdi o meu chapéu," said the mouse.

Mr and Mrs Frog could not speak Portuguese. They had no idea what the little mouse was saying.

What shall we do? they wondered.

Maybe she's lost an umbrella. Everyone loses an umbrella at least twice, thought Mr Frog.

"Have you lost this?" asked Mr Frog.

"Um guarda-chuva? Não," replied the mouse.

Then Mrs Frog remembered something that had been handed in a few months ago...

"Is this yours?" Mrs Frog asked, holding up a chunk of cheese.

"Queijo? Não. Isto fede!" said the mouse.

"Time to put that cheese in the bin dear," said Mr Frog.

"Maybe the word 'chapéu' means coat," said Mr Frog.

"Now where did I put that nice yellow one?"

"Got it!" said Mr Frog.

"Um casaco? Não. Perdi o meu chapéu," said the mouse.

She was starting to feel a bit frustrated.

"We need to keep trying," said Mrs Frog.

Não é um lenço.

Não são calças.

Não é uma camisola.

Nem óculos de sol.

Não são sapatos.

"Perdi o meu chapéu," said the mouse.

Nem duas bicicletas.

Não é um computador.

Não são três livros.

Nem quatro bananas.

Nem cinco chaves.

It was no good. A fat wet tear rolled
down the mouse's cheek.

"How about a nice cup of tea?" asked Mrs Frog kindly.

"Eu adoro chá. Obrigado," replied the mouse. They sat together, sipping their tea and all feeling a bit sad.

Suddenly, the mouse realised she could try pointing.

She pointed at her head.
"Chapéu!" she said.

"I've got it!" exclaimed Mrs Frog, leaping up.

"A wig of course!" said Mrs Frog.

"Não é uma peruca," said the mouse.

Não é vermelha.

Não é loira.

Não é castanha.

Não é multicolorida.

Não é verde.

"What about this?"
asked Mr Frog, pulling back
a curtain.

"Chapéu!" exclaimed
the mouse.

"Ah, so 'chapéu' means hat.
Wonderful!" Mr and Mrs
Frog cheered.

Muito alto.

Demasiado pequeno.

Demasiado grande.

Demasiado apertado.

"One hat left," said Mrs Frog, reaching all the way to the back of the cupboard.

"It couldn't be this old thing, could it?"

"O meu chapéu.

Encontrei o meu chapéu!

Muito obrigado," said the mouse.

And just like that, the mouse found her hat.

"Adeus," she said, as she skipped away.
"Adeus," replied Mr and Mrs Frog.

"I wonder who will come tomorrow?" said Mr Frog.
Mrs Frog put her arm around him.

"I don't know," she replied, giving him a squeeze,
"but whoever it is, we'll do our best to help."

LEARNING TO LOVE LANGUAGES

An additional language opens a child's mind, broadens their horizons and enriches their emotional life. Research has shown that the time between a child's birth and their sixth or seventh birthday is a "golden period" when they are most receptive to new languages. This is because they have an in-built ability to distinguish the sounds they hear and make sense of them. The Story-powered Language Learning Method taps into these natural abilities.

HOW THE STORY-POWERED LANGUAGE LEARNING METHOD WORKS

We create an emotionally engaging and funny story for children and adults to enjoy together, just like any other picture book. Studies show that social interaction, like enjoying a book together, is critical in language learning.

Through the story, we introduce a relatable character who speaks only in the new language. This helps build empathy and a positive attitude towards people who speak different languages. These are both important aspects in laying the foundations for lasting language acquisition in a child's life.

As the story progresses, the child naturally works with the characters to discover the meaning of a wide range of fun new words. Strategic use of humour ensures that this subconscious learning is rewarded with laughter; the child feels good and the first seeds of a lifelong love of languages are sown.

For more information and free downloads visit www.neuwestendpress.com

ALL THE BEAUTIFUL PORTUGUESE WORDS AND PHRASES FROM OUR STORY

perdi o meu chapéu	I've lost my hat
um guarda-chuva	an umbrella
queijo	cheese
isto fede	it stinks
um casaco	a coat
um lenço	a scarf
calças	trousers
óculos de sol	sunglasses
camisola	sweater
sapatos	shoes
um	one
dois	two
três	three
quatro	four
cinco	five
computador	computer
livros	books
chaves	keys
bananas	bananas
bicicletas	bicycles
eu adoro chá	I love tea
obrigado	thank you
peruca	wig
vermelha	red (f)
loira	blond (f)
castanha	brown (f)

verde	green (f)
multicolorida	multicoloured
chapéu	hat
muito alto	too tall
demasiado grande	too big
demasiado pequeno	too small
demasiado apertado	too tight
encontrei o meu chapéu	I've found my hat
muito obrigado	thank you very much
adeus	goodbye

THE WORLD OF
THE FABULOUS LOST & FOUND

THIS STORY IS ALSO AVAILABLE IN...

FRENCH   SPANISH

ITALIAN   CZECH

WELSH

KOREAN   GERMAN   HEBREW

SWEDISH   POLISH   SLOVAKIAN

VIETNAMESE   LATIN   TAGALOG

...AND MANY MORE LANGUAGES!

ENJOYED IT?
WRITE A REVIEW AND
LET US KNOW!

@MARK_PALLIS ON TWITTER
WWW.MARKPALLIS.COM

@PETERBAYNTON ON INSTAGRAM
WWW.PETERBAYNTON.COM

Printed in Great Britain
by Amazon

33131146R00023